ETERNAL LIFE!
Believe To Be Alive

WORKBOOK

Free Grace International
2 Circle Rd.
Longview TX, 75602

Copyright © 2019 Free Grace International 2 Circle Rd, Longview, TX 75602 Published by FREEGRACE.IN

© Copyright by Lucas Kitchen Text and design by Lucas Kitchen

Project Editor: John Goodding, Additional design: Kristah Kitchen. Published by FREE GRACE INTERNATIONAL

NEW KING JAMES VERSION (NKJV): Scripture taken from the NEW KING JAMES VERSION®. Copyright© 1982 by Thomas Nelson, Inc. Used by permission. All rights reserved.

NEW INTERNATIONAL VERSION (NIV): Scripture taken from THE HOLY BIBLE, NEW INTERNATIONAL VERSION ®. Copyright© 1973, 1978, 1984, 2011 by Biblica, Inc.™. Used by permission of Zondervan

HOLY BIBLE, NEW LIVING TRANSLATION (NLT): Scriptures taken from the HOLY BIBLE, NEW LIVING TRANSLATION, Copyright© 1996, 2004, 2007 by Tyndale House Foundation. Used by permission of Tyndale House Publishers, Inc., Carol Stream, Illinois 60188. All rights reserved. Used by permission.

TABLE OF CONTENTS

SESSION 1: THE OBLIVIOUS 7
SESSION 2: THE OBSESSION 13
SESSION 3: THE OBLIGATION 19
SESSION 4: THE OBJECT 23
SESSION 5: THE OBJECTIVE 27
SESSION 6: THE ONUS 35
SESSION 7: THE OBVIOUS 45

ACCESS THE FREE EXPANDED CONTENT

This workbook is the companion study for the book *Eternal Life: Believe To Be Alive*. To purchase copies of *Eternal Life* or to access the free media that goes with this book scan the code with your device's camera or visit the web address below. FREEGRACE.IN/EL

THE OBLIVIOUS
Section One:

Read Chapters **1** *and* **2** *in Eternal Life*

Could you relate to the confusion expressed in the first two chapters of the book? If so explain.

How have you seen confusion and disagreement effect your church, and the church in general?

Tell about a time you heard a Bible teacher, leader or pastor deliver an unclear Gospel message?

SALVATION SURVEY

WHAT'S YOUR CHURCH BACKGROUND? (MULTIPLE IS OK)

- ☐ Baptist
- ☐ Methodist
- ☐ Catholic
- ☐ Lutheran
- ☐ Presbyterian
- ☐ Pentecostal
- ☐ 7th Day Adventist
- ☐ Church of Christ
- ☐ Mormon
- ☐ Universalism
- ☐ Free Grace
- ☐ Non-Denominational
- ☐ Jehovah's Witness
- ☐ Bible Church
- ☐ Episcopal
- ☐ Orthodox
- ☐ Anglican
- ☐ Other

WHAT IS YOUR EXPERIENCE WITH THE CHRISTIAN FAITH?

- ☐ None
- ☐ Average
- ☐ Experienced (I read my Bible regularly),
- ☐ Volunteer Teacher/Church Leader (Sunday school, Bible study, etc.)
- ☐ Minister (vocational, bi-vocational, or volunteer)

WHICH OF THESE IS REQUIRED FOR SOMEONE TO BE ETERNALLY SAVED?

- ☐ Ask Jesus into your heart
- ☐ Accept Jesus as your Lord and Savior
- ☐ Pray a sinners prayer
- ☐ Believe In Jesus (for everlasting life)
- ☐ Make a commitment to follow Jesus
- ☐ Understand that you are a sinner
- ☐ Confess that Jesus is Lord
- ☐ Ask for forgiveness of sins
- ☐ Love Jesus
- ☐ Be baptized
- ☐ Believe that Jesus died on the Cross for your sins
- ☐ Believe that Jesus rose from the dead
- ☐ Repent of your sins
- ☐ Call upon the name of the Lord
- ☐ Take Communion
- ☐ Go and sin no more
- ☐ Bear fruit
- ☐ Take up your cross daily
- ☐ Be a disciple
- ☐ Follow Christ
- ☐ Place your faith in Christ
- ☐ Endure/persevere until the end
- ☐ Abide in Christ
- ☐ Have good works
- ☐ Have a relationship with Jesus
- ☐ Experience life change
- ☐ I don't know

Read Chapters **3** *and* **4** *in Eternal Life*

How did taking the survey make you feel?

How likely do you think other Christians would be to agree with what you put on the survey? Why?

Did the low percentage of agreement on the requirement for salvation surprise you? In what way?

PERCENTAGE OF AGREEMENT
On the requirements of salvation

Requirement	%
Take Communion	4%
Have Good Works	4%
Go And Sin No More	9%
Experience Life Change	10%
Bear Fruit	10%
Be Baptized	12%
Pray A Sinner's Prayer	15%
Be A Disciple	16%
Take Up Your Cross Daily	17%
Endure/persevere Until The End	17%
Abide In Christ	19%
Call Upon The Name Of The Lord	28%
Ask Jesus Into Your Heart	31%
Love Jesus	32%
Follow Christ	38%
Make A Commitment To Follow Jesus	40%
Have A Relationship With Jesus	44%
Place Your Faith In Christ	44%
Ask For Forgiveness Of Sins	51%
Understand That You Are A Sinner	58%
Repent Of Your Sins	60%
Confess That Jesus Is Lord	60%
Believe That Jesus Rose From The Dead	67%
Believe In Jesus For Everlasting Life	72%
Accept Jesus As Your Lord And Savior	73%
Believe That Jesus Died For Your Sins	77%

100%

8 ETERNAL LIFE

Read Chapters **5** *and* **6** *in Eternal Life*

> "If you knew the gift of God, and who it is who says to you, 'Give Me a drink,' you would have asked Him, and He would have given you living water." John 4:10

Why is it significant that Jesus calls the saving message "living water"?

What do you think it is that has muddied the living water and why has this happened?

THE OBLIVIOUS

THE OBSESSION
Section Two:

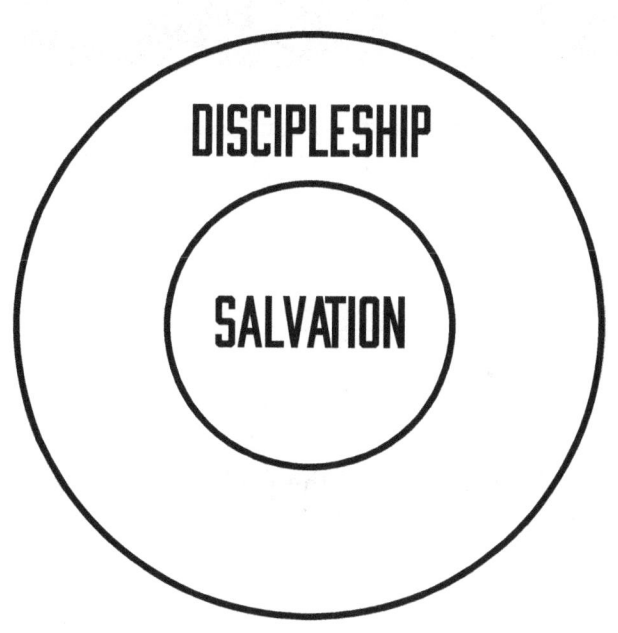

Read Chapters **7** *and* **8** *in Eternal Life*

What is your favorite verse for telling someone how to have eternal life? Why is this your favorite?

> All Scripture is given by inspiration of God, and is profitable for doctrine, for reproof, for correction, for instruction in righteousness, that the man of God may be complete, thoroughly equipped for every good work. 2 Timothy 3:16-17

How could this verse affect your view of the purpose for the Bible?

What do think of this statement? "Many books of the Bible point to eternal life, but few give specific instructions on how to receive it."

Read Chapters **9** *and* **10** *in Eternal Life*

> And truly Jesus did many other signs in the presence of His disciples, which are not written in this book; but these are written that you may believe that Jesus is the Christ, the Son of God, and that believing you may have life in His name. John 20:30-31

Based on John 20:30-31, what is the purpose of John's Gospel?

Why is it significant that John is so clear on the purpose of his Gospel?

According to the verse above, what does someone have to do to "have life in His name"?

Read Chapter **11** *in Eternal Life*

> And Jesus came and spoke to them, saying, "All authority has been given to Me in heaven and on earth. Go therefore and make disciples of all the nations, baptizing them in the name of the Father and of the Son and of the Holy Spirit, teaching them to observe all things that I have commanded you;" Matthew 28:18-20

What is the purpose of the book of Matthew according to 28:18-20?

> I also have decided to write an accurate account for you, most honorable Theophilus, so you can be certain of the truth of everything you were taught. Luke 1:3-4

What do we learn about the audience and purpose of the book of Luke from this verse?

The book of Acts is also written to Theophilus. What does that tell us about its audience and purpose?

Read Chapter **12** *in Eternal Life*

How does the chart help to explain the purpose and intended use of the books in the Bible?

How should this affect our approach to evangelism?

THE PURPOSE
CIRCLES
Of the Bible

DISCIPLESHIP
The Entire Bible

SALVATION
Gospel Of John

THE OBLIGATION
Section Three:

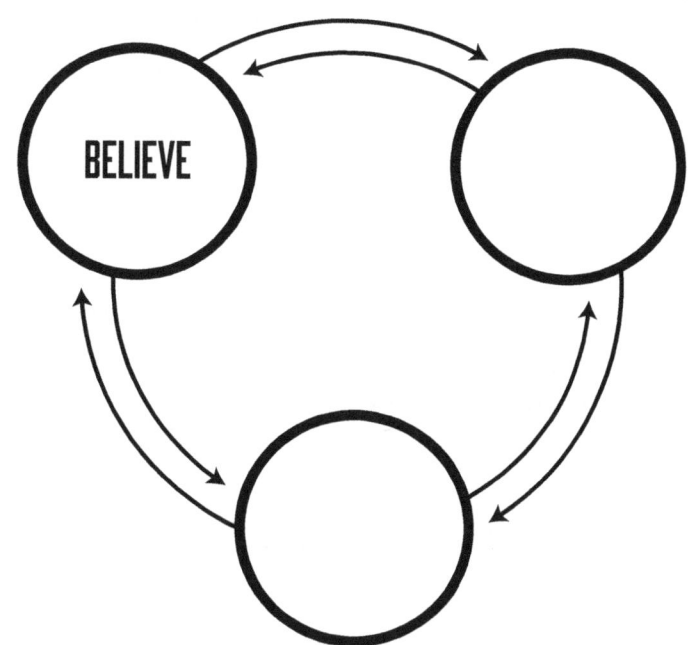

Read Chapters **13** *and* **14** *in Eternal Life*

Why is it significant that the word believe is used so many times in the Gospel of John, and not as much in other books of the Bible?

What definitions for the word believe have you heard used?

Why does it matter how the word believe is defined?

Read Chapter **15** *in Eternal Life*

How is the word believe used in the Gospel of John?

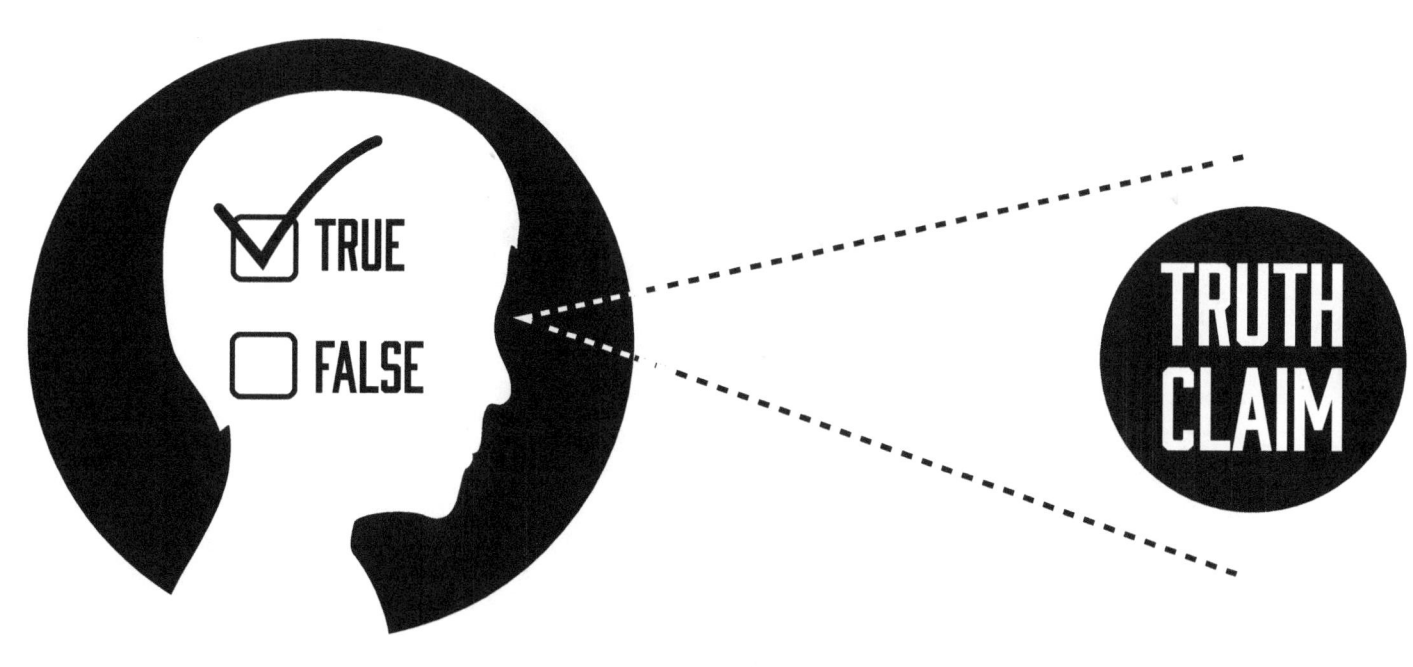

THE OBLIGATION 19

THE OBJECT
Section Four:

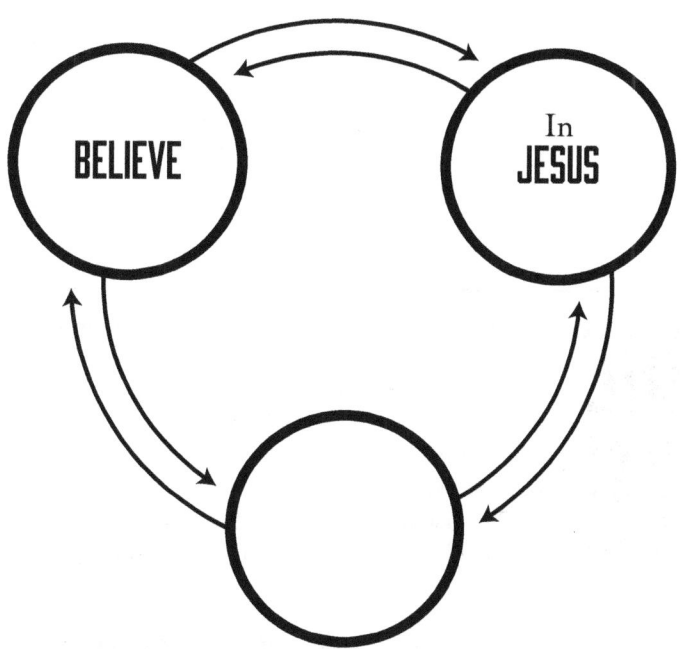

Read Chapters **16** *and* **17** *in Eternal Life*

> And there are also many other things that Jesus did, which if they were written one by one, I suppose that even the world itself could not contain the books that would be written. John 21:25

Why do you think John used the specific accounts of Jesus' life that he did in the Gospel of John?

_____
_____
_____
_____

How might the time line below, change the thinking some may have on what must be believed to have eternal life?

_____
_____
_____
_____
_____

1. John the Baptist announces Jesus' identity in public. (1:34)
2. Andrew and John spend the day together with Jesus. (1:37-39)
3. A few disciples believe in Jesus for salvation. (1:41,45,49)
4. The other disciples believe in Jesus for salvation. (2:11)
5. Peter reaffirms the disciple's belief in Jesus. (6:68)
6. The disciples learn that Jesus knows everything. (16:30)
7. The disciples learn that Jesus rose from the dead. (20:1-29)
8. They learn what Jesus meant by raising the temple. (2:22)

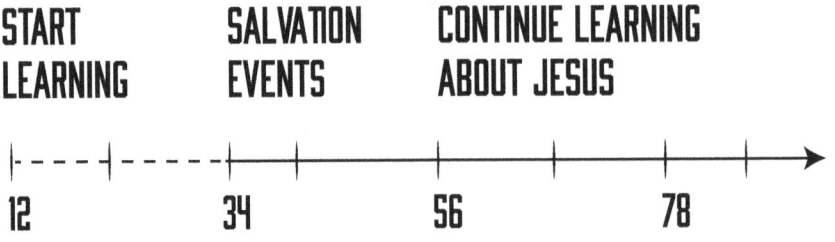

22 ETERNAL LIFE

Gospel presentations can include many truths from the Bible. List some of the truths about Jesus that you have heard in Gospel presentations?

Which of these truths must be believed to have eternal life?

Read Chapters **19** *in Eternal Life*

What are some of your favorite names and titles for Jesus?

What do these titles convey about Jesus?

Which names or titles demonstrate He is able to give eternal life?

MESSIAH
Messiah is coming...
(4:25a)

IS

CHRIST
...who is called Christ.
(4:25b)

IS

SON OF GOD
...the Christ, the Son of God... (11:27)

IS

SAVIOR
...the Christ, the Savior of the world. (4:42)

IS

Read Chapters **19** *in Eternal Life*

> Jesus said to her [Martha], "I am the resurrection and the life. He who believes in Me, though he may die, he shall live. And whoever lives and believes in Me shall never die. Do you believe this?" She said to Him, "Yes, Lord, I believe that You are the Christ, the Son of God, who is to come into the world." John 11:25-27

How does Jesus' explanation of his ability relate to Martha's description of his identity?

In these verses what specific things does someone need to believe in order to experience resurrection and life?

Why is it significant that Jesus asks Martha "Do you believe this?"

THE OBJECT 25

THE OBJECTIVE
Section Five:

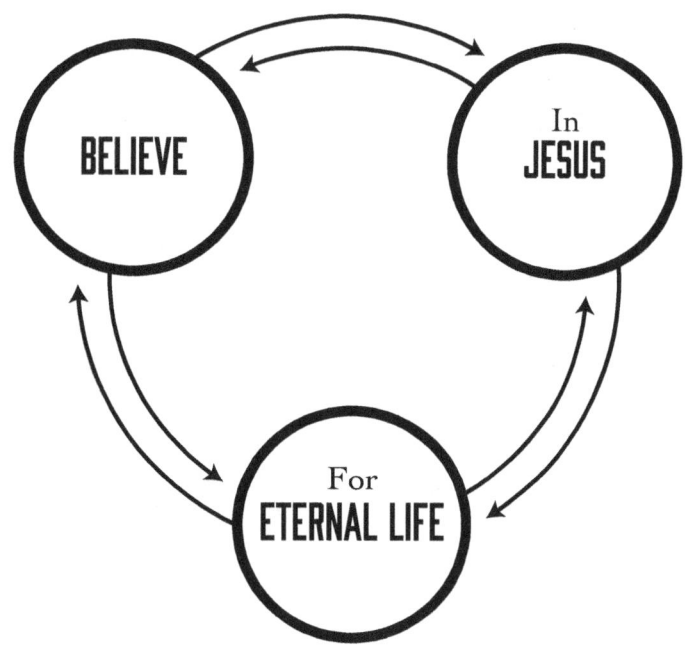

Read Chapter **20** *in Eternal Life*

The objective for believing in Jesus is to have eternal life. What are some other objectives or reasons some people have believed in Jesus for?

What are some synonyms you've heard used for eternal life?

How would you define eternal life?

Read Chapter **21** *in Eternal Life*

> He who believes in the Son has everlasting life; and he who does not believe the Son shall not see life, but the wrath of God abides on him. John 3:36

According to the verse above what does a person have to do to receive eternal life?

What do you think it means for the wrath of God to abide on a person in this verse?

Why do you think John used death instead of hell to describe eternal separation from God?

Read Chapter **22** *in Eternal Life*

Why do you think the requirement of good works get added to Gospel presentations so often?

What are some examples of prerequisite and postrequisite works being added to the Gospel?

Read Chapter **23** *in Eternal Life*

> And I give them eternal life, and they shall never perish; neither shall anyone snatch them out of My hand. My Father, who has given them to Me, is greater than all; and no one is able to snatch them out of My Father's hand. John 10:28-29

How does this verse help in understanding eternal life?

Based on this verse, how would you respond to a person who said you could lose eternal life if you stopped believing?

THE OBJECTIVE 31

Read Chapter **24** *in Eternal Life*

> "Most assuredly, I say to you, he who hears My word and believes in Him who sent Me has everlasting life, and shall not come into judgment, but has passed from death into life." John 5:24

What must one do to receive the benefits mentioned in this verse?

Explain the past present and future effects of believing in Jesus according to this verse.

IF YOU HAVE BELIEVED *in Jesus for eternal life.*

YOU

- Passed from death into life. — **PAST**
- Have eternal life. — **PRESENT**
- Will not come into judgment. — **FUTURE**

How might it effect a person if they do not understand the past, present and future effects of eternal life?

32 ETERNAL LIFE

Read Chapter  *in Eternal Life*

> I am the way, the truth, and the life. No one comes to the Father except through Me.
> John 14:6

By what 'other' methods do people attempt to reach Heaven, and God?

How does the diagram below relate to this verse?

BELIEVE IN

- Jesus + Works → **RECEIVE NOTHING**
- Jesus + Nothing → **RECEIVE ETERNAL LIFE**
- Works + Nothing → **RECEIVE NOTHING**

THE OBJECTIVE 33

SEVEN SALVATION STATEMENTS
In the Gospel of John

OBLIGATION		OBJECT	OBJECTIVE
Whoever believes	in	Him	shall not perish but have eternal life.
whoever believes	in	Him	shall not perish but have everlasting life.
He who believes	in	the Son	has everlasting life …
everyone who sees the Son and believes	in	Him	may have everlasting life…
he who believes	in	Me	has everlasting life.
He who believes	in	Me	though he may die, he shall live.
that you may believe	that	Jesus is the Christ, the Son of God,	and that believing you may have life in His name.

In Vertical Order: John 3:15, 3:16, 3:36, 6:40, 6:47, 11:25-26, 20:30-31

What is significant about the OBLIGATION column on the chart?

What is significant about the OBJECT column on the chart?

What is significant about the OBJECTIVE column on the chart?

What does the chart prove about Jesus' method for receiving salvation?

THE ONUS
Section Six:

Read Chapters **26** *and* **27** *in Eternal Life*

What do you think about the statement "It's Jesus' job to convince you to believe in Him for eternal life"?

How great an impact do you think John the Baptist's testimony about Jesus being the Christ, had on the people of that time? What impact should it have on us?

Read Chapter **28** *in Eternal Life*

> Believe Me that I am in the Father and the Father in Me, or else believe Me for the sake of the works themselves. John 14:11

What do you think about the idea that Jesus' miracles where constructive rather than destructive?

_____
_____
_____
_____
_____
_____

How do the miracles listed in the diagram provide proof that Jesus is the Christ?

_____
_____
_____
_____
_____
_____
_____
_____
_____
_____
_____
_____
_____
_____
_____

THE TWENTY ONE SIGNS
In the Gospel of John

Turns Water Into Wine	(2:1-11)
Prophesies His Resurrection	(2:19-20)
Prophesies Woman's Deeds	(4:18-19)
Heals The Royal Man's Son	(4:46-54)
Heals The Paralytic Man	(5:1-15)
Feeds A Group Of 5000+	(6:5-14)
Walks On Stormy Waters	(6:16-24)
Moves The Boat To Shore	(6:21)
Heals The Blind Man	(9:1-7)
Raises Lazarus From Dead	(11:1-45)
Prophesies His Own Death	(12:32-33)
Prophesies Judas' Betrayal	(13:25-26)
Prophesies Peter's Denial	(13:38)
Knocks The Soldiers Down	(18:6)
Leaves The Grave Empty	(20:3-8)
Appears First To Mary	(20:14-16)
Appears To Ten Disciples	(20:19-20)
Appears to Thomas	(20:26-27)
Appears to The Seven	(21:4-5)
Gives A Great Fishing Tip	(21:6)
Prophesies Peter's Death	(21:18-19)

THE ONUS

Read Chapter **29** *in Eternal Life*

> Look, the Lamb of God, who takes away the sin of the world! John 1:29
>
> He is the atoning sacrifice for our sins, and not only for ours but also for the sins of the whole world. 1 John 2:2

Whose sins were paid for on the cross?

How important was Christ's death on the cross?

How does Christ's death prove He is who says He is?

Read Chapters **30** *and* **31** *in Eternal Life*

> And if Christ has not been raised, then our preaching is in vain and your faith is in vain.
> 1 Corinthians 15:14

What does this verse tell us about the importance of Christ's resurrection?

How is Christ's resurrection and our coming resurrection related?

> Father, glorify your name." Then a voice came from heaven: "I have glorified it, and I will glorify it again." The crowd that stood there and heard it said that it had thundered. Others said, "An angel has spoken to him." Jesus answered, "This voice has come for your sake, not mine. John 12:28-30

What impact do you think it would have had on you to be there and hear this conversation between God the Father and His Son?

Read Chapter **32** *in Eternal Life*

> "If I bear witness of Myself, My witness is not true. There is another who bears witness of Me, and I know that the witness which He witnesses of Me is true. You have sent to John, and he has borne witness to the truth. But I have a greater witness than John's; for the works which the Father has given Me to finish—the very works that I do—bear witness of Me, that the Father has sent Me. And the Father Himself, who sent Me, has testified of Me. You search the Scriptures, for in them you think you have eternal life; and these are they which testify of Me. But you are not willing to come to Me that you may have life.
> John 5:31, 32, 36, 39, 40

What four witnesses are listed in these verses?

What is the significance and impact of these witnesses?

There are well over 200 prophecies about Christ in the Old Testament. What are some of your favorites?

Read Chapter **33** *in Eternal Life*

What are some of the prophecies Christ made that have been fulfilled?

How does the fact that Jesus was a prophet provide further proof that He is the Christ?

Read Chapter **34** *in Eternal Life*

> The light has come into the world, and men loved darkness rather than light, because their deeds were evil. John 3:19
>
> ...You are not willing to come to Me that you may have life. John 5:40

What reasons have you heard people give for not believing the Gospel?

What reason does Jesus give in the verses above for people's refusal to believe?

How should you respond if someone refuses to believe in Jesus?

BEING FULLY CONVINCED
by the evidence.

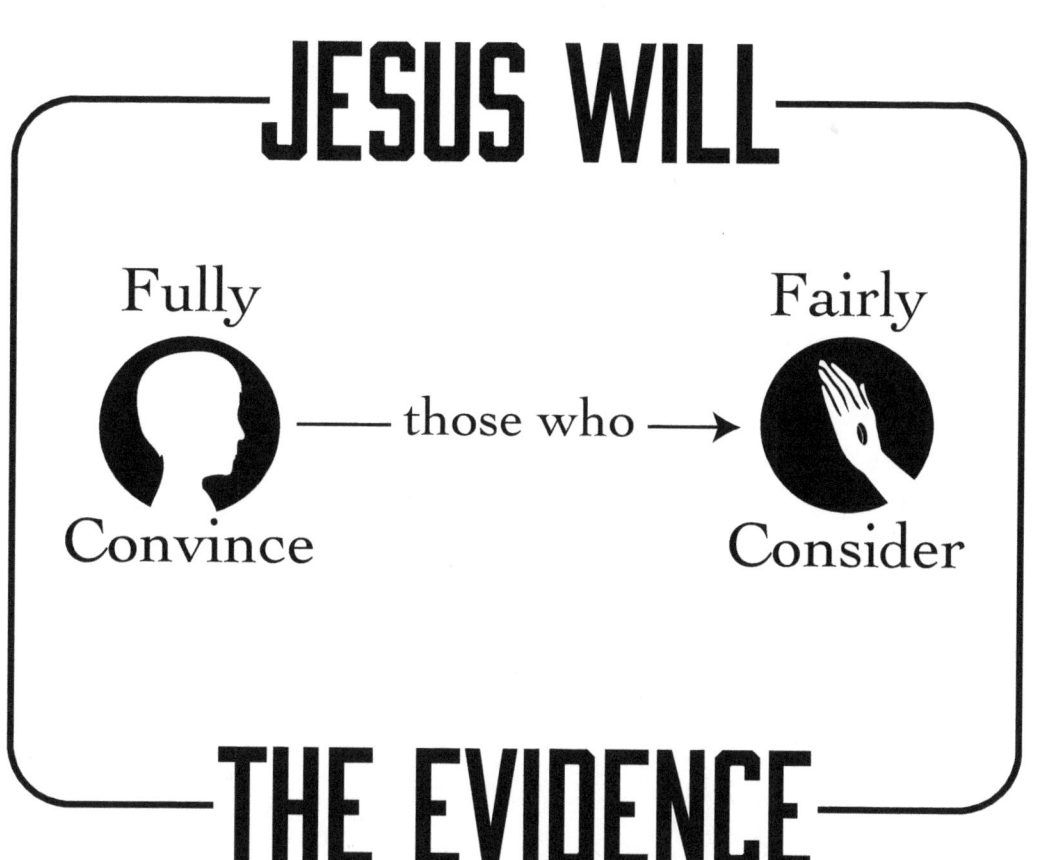

THE OBVIOUS
Section Seven:

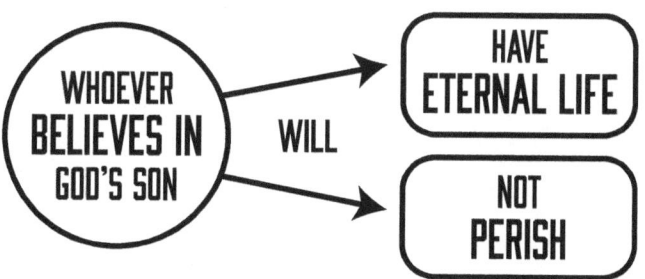

Read Chapters **35** *and* **36** *in Eternal Life*

How might using this John 3:16 diagram help you share the Gospel in the future?

_____
_____
_____
_____

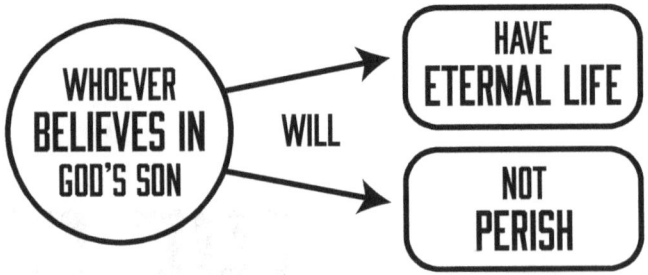

In the space below, practice drawing the John 3:16 diagram as you talk through the verse. You can refer to the explanation in the book *Eternal Life* (pg. 264). Use the draw order key to make your drawing.

> For God so loved the world that He gave His only begotten Son, that whoever believes in Him should not perish but have everlasting life. John 3:16

DRAW ORDER
1. World (circle)
2. Whoever
3. Perish
4. God's Son
5. Believes in
6. Will
7. Not (Perish)
8. Have eternal life

Read Chapters **37** *and* **38** *in Eternal Life*

How do you think these questions might help you know if someone understands the Gospel?

Are there additional questions you may want to ask someone you are sharing the Gospel with to ensure they understand?

> **7 QUESTIONS**
>
> 1. Do you know for sure that you will go to heaven?
>
> 2. How many of your sins did Jesus die for on the cross?
>
> 3. What is the only thing god asks you to do to gain everlasting life?
>
> 4. How long does everlasting life last?
>
> 5. When does your everlasting life begin?
>
> 6. Do you believe in Jesus for everlasting life?
>
> 7. If you were to do something really bad and then die, would you go to heaven or hell? Why?

THE OBVIOUS

For more materials from the FGI team visit:

FREEGRACE.IN

Please share what you've learned!